WHERE DO WISHES GO?

For my Mother and Father,
who inspired a love of books – DB

For my sister, Gem – JM

Text copyright © Debra Bertulis 2022
Illustrations copyright © Jess Mason 2022

First published in Great Britain and in the USA in 2022 by
Otter-Barry Books, Little Orchard, Burley Gate,
Herefordshire, HR1 3QS
www.otterbarrybooks.com

A catalogue record for this book is available from the British Library

Designed by Arianna Osti

FSC
www.fsc.org
MIX
Paper from
responsible sources
FSC® C018072

ISBN 978-1-91307-439-5

Illustrated with digital media

Set in Calibri

Printed in the United Kingdom

9 8 7 6 5 4 3 2 1

WHERE DO WISHES GO?

Poems by
Debra Bertulis

Illustrations by Jess Mason

Otter-Barry BOOKS

Contents

Poems Are Doors

Poems are doors, there to unlock
You already have the key
Sit down with one in a cosy nook
Then you will see what I mean

Be prepared for magic
Ready for a thunderous ride
Riding a silver-maned unicorn
With moonlight as your guide

Dance in the forest with fairies
Swim in the ocean with whales
Fly to the stars or walk on the moon
Follow the mystery trail

Poetry transports you
Over land and air and sea
Find your poetry door today
You already have the key

Greedy Gull!

He eyes
He spies
He swoops

He dips

There goes the last
Of my fish and chips!

Witches' Brew for All the Family

Abracadabra
Kalamalace...
Mum's mobile phone
Her make-up case
Abracadabra
Kalamazar...
Dad's bad jokes
His embarrassing car
Abracadabra
Kalamazits...
Sister's homework
Her itchy nits
Abracadabra
Kalamazeet...
Brother's trainers
His pongy feet
Abracadabra
Kalamazock...
My school uniform
My alarm clock
Abracadabra
Kalamatall...
Smell of wet dog
His squeakiest ball

Abracadabra
Kalamazi...
Boiled cabbage
Broccoli
Abracadabra
Kalamazoo...
Quick!
Run away
Before I choose

YOU!

Miss Jazz

Whenever Miss Jazz
walks towards us in town,
Mum lowers her eyes,
diverts them down.

She hurries me past
though I just want to stare
at this work of art,
at her style and flair.

A felt patchwork hat
of orange and red
rests neatly on top
of her violet head.

A long floaty dress
of purple and blue
with a sparkling belt
makes a dazzling view.

She's matched her earrings,
the exact same shade
as the stripes in her tights,
blue, pink and jade.

A long chiffon scarf
patterned yellow and green,
Miss Jazz is a prism,
a Kaleidoscope Queen.

From the hat on her head
to the shoes on her toes,
Miss Jazz spreads a rainbow
wherever she goes!

Heart

There is a HEART inside
EARTH
Can you find it?

Falling Apart

I heard Mum say
she's falling apart,
but she looks OK to me.
Her head's still on her shoulders
with two arms,
two legs,
two knees.

She says she'll be all right,
that she'll pull herself together.
I'm not to worry, not to fret,
she's just a bit under the weather.

Last time I checked she was still intact,
it's a mystery to me.
So, I think I'll read her a story
and make her a cup of tea.

.

Grandad's Leaving Home

Will Grandad need a suitcase
When he goes to heaven?
Will he need a crisp white shirt
To dress for dinner at seven?

Will he need his passport
For city breaks away?
Will God let him use a phone
To ring us every day?

Will he know which peg is his
To hang his coat and hat?
Will he be shown where the toilets are
And important things like that?

Will there be a watchman
Who stays awake all night?
Will he know that Grandad
Can't sleep without a light?

Will God give him money
To buy a paper and sweets?
And his ticket to the football
The highlight of his week?

Will He notice if he's sad
And listen to his fears?
Will somebody care enough
To wipe away his tears?

Who is listening to me now?
Is anybody there?
I hope that God has taken notes
And won't forget this prayer.

Star City

Dear Mum and Dad,
I'm off to Star City in Russia
to train as an astronaut.
Saved up all my pocket money.
You should see the space suit I bought!
I'll float in the air upside-down
and get used to weightlessness,
spin in a giant washing machine
in a centrifugal mess!
There's not much room in a spacecraft,
so sorry you can't come too.
It's cramped and full of screens and lights,
just room for me and the crew.
I've been chosen for my bravery,
my scientific brain.
I am the one they want –
I hope we will meet again.
So, this is goodbye,
over and out
from your astronaut child (that's me).
Just one thing before I fly...

What are you having for tea?

Star City is a real place in Russia, home to the Yuri Gagarin Cosmonaut Training Centre.
Astronauts train there, although in Russia astronauts are called 'cosmonauts'. It's built like a real city with banks, schools, theatres, cinemas, even its own railway station!

Poetry Potty!

(For pupils and staff of Bengeworth CE Primary Academy, Evesham, which is an Official Poetry Potty School!)

We're poetry potty
At this school
Poetry is everywhere
Poetry rules!

A shape poem for breakfast
Ooh, what a treat!
Watch it swirl down the page
Good enough to eat!

We're poetry potty
Potty! Potty! Potty!
Poetry potty
At this school!

A haiku for snack
Three lines of these
Or a sonnet perhaps
Fourteen lines, please!

We're poetry potty
Potty! Potty! Potty!
Poetry potty
At this school!

A kenning for lunch
Or a ballad, perhaps?
Cinquain for pudding
With our poetry chat!

We're poetry potty
Potty! Potty! Potty!
Poetry potty
At this school!

Acrostic at playtime
Spell out your name
Or make rhyme with your time
Make poetry a game!

We're poetry potty
Potty! Potty! Potty!
Poetry potty
At this school!
(Repeat!)

Looking After Mum

Wake
Check on Mum
Dress
Hang washing out
Load washer
Check on Mum
Wake sister
Cup of tea for Mum
Medication for Mum
Put Mum's phone by her bed
Chivvy sister
Toast for Mum
Do sister's plaits
Toast for sister
Wash up
Check sister's PE kit
Check on Mum
Grab bag
Grab keys
Call goodbye to Mum
Rumbling tummy
Run!
Empty playground
Sign in at Reception
See sister into Class

Thinking about Mum
Open the door to my Class
Twenty-nine stares
Hang up coat quickly!
Find seat
Breathe
Focus
Try
Try
Not to worry about
Mum

Hair-Scare!

If a visit to the hairdresser
Does not go as it should
Make sure you wear your coat to school
The one which has
A HOOD!

Fly In My Soup!

Waiter! Waiter!
There's a fly in my soup,
one that I did not request.
By the looks of it
it is deceased,
and not just taking a rest.

Bury it, waiter,
give it respect.
The fly's not to blame,
he fell in, I suspect.

Though this sort of thing
is incredibly rare,
please tell your chef
to cook with more care!

Mike the Mirror

This is the tale
Of Mike the Mirror
Who could find his reflection
In a concrete pillar

Mike the Mirror
So in love with his face
Sought his reflection
All over the place

Shoppers would smile
As they heard him shout
"Is that me in that window?
Or is James Bond about?"

Then they'd "Ooh" and "Aah"
As he found his reflection
Put his lips to the glass
To no one's objection

Some years later
Mike went missing
He'd dissolved himself
In a pool of kisses

Mike the Mirror
Was so sorely missed
The town built a statue
Of Mike blowing a kiss

Blowing a kiss to shoppers
Who pay their respects each day
To the man called Mike the Mirror
Who kissed himself away.

New Boy

I have come from another land
Where life was not always good
Where people weren't happy
Where people weren't kind
They didn't behave as they should

I have come from another land
With Mum and my baby brother
My dad, my sister
Uncles and aunts
We all look after each other

I have come from another land
Your land is my land now
I'm learning your language
Learning to smile
New friends are teaching me how

I have come from another land
To your land where people are free
Where people are happy
Where people are kind
Where people are just like me.

All the Days

Sometimes
the sky is a palette of sadness,
blacks and greys of all shades.
A let's-run-home-before-it-rains day!

Sometimes
that same sky
is a sailing ship.
Climb aboard!
Follow those clouds for miles.
A dream-away-the-hours day!

Sometimes
there are mountains to climb,
a slow, heavy trudge to the top.
A pick-me-up-and-carry-me-please day!

Sometimes
those same mountains are
shadows
that I skip in and out of.
A glad-to-be-alive day!

What will tomorrow bring?

Gran's Cat

My Gran and her cat
love to chat.
She says,
"Come in,
lie by the fire.
I wouldn't want to be out
in this weather,
scampering up trees."

Cat asks
Where would you choose to climb
If you were me?

"Oh, I'd choose a sunny day
with a warm breeze.
I'd sit at the top of
a sycamore or beech,
look out over the fields
of sunflowers,
bowing their heads
to the day."

Gran says,
"What shall we have for supper?
Shall I open a can of tuna
or would you prefer some meat?"

Cat asks
What would you choose to eat
If you were me?

"Ooh, I'd hang around the Fish Man
until he closed up,
feast on the tastiest scraps
of sardines, salmon and trout.
Oh, yes, my belly would ache
with bliss."

Gran says,
"You've found a nice spot there,
stretched out in the sun.
You'll bake yourself
if you're not careful."

Cat asks
Where would you sit
If you were me?

"On the highest red roof,
looking out across Florence,
watching the sun set in a crimson sky
over the olive groves
and lemon trees beyond.
Lulled to sleep
by the bells of the town.

How about that, Cat?"

Cat says

Ooh, yes
But the best ever place
A cat could be
Is snuggled in your lap
Warmed by the flames of a fire
Dreaming of nothing at all.

Jack's Mountain

Jack was obsessed with Mount Everest.
The shelves in his bedroom were stacked
with books of the earliest expeditions.
Hillary and Tenzing were obvious heroes
but Jack's admiration for mountaineers
George Mallory and Andrew Irvine
stretched way beyond anything.
I can see him now, crouched on his floor,
book open at another page of black-and-white
    photographs,
eyes glistening with passion, with a voice I never
    heard in school,
talking about his own dream to climb Everest,
how Mallory was found without his wife's picture
    he'd vowed to leave at the summit.
Irvine and his camera were still missing.
The Northeast Ridge was the last sighting of the men,
    just below the top.
Had they reached the summit?
Or never reached it at all?

Jack moved to another school far away from the
    taunts of his bullies.
Someone else listens to him now, no doubt with the
    same intensity as me.
And it would come as no surprise
if, one day in the future, I hear about a quiet man
    named Jack
who reached the summit of Mount Everest,
spurred on by the spirit of his heroes
and, on his descent,
discovered the missing
Andrew Irvine.

What happened to the photograph of Mallory's wife?
Where is the missing camera?
Where exactly is Andrew 'Sandy' Irvine's final resting place?
If just one these questions were answered, it could solve what many
believe is the biggest mountaineering mystery of all time.

Thinking Place

There is nothing like finding
Somewhere quiet
To have a really good think
Away from everything
The kind of think
That stretches into dreams

To Be a Tree

I'm a tree
Again
In the school play
Trees don't talk
They just stand in the way
I'm bored
I'm embarrassed
Under these leaves
Is the reddest face
You'll ever see
But I have a plan
To wink from inside
Catch Mum's eye
Watch her beam with pride
Then I'll shiver and shake
I'll sway a bit too
Play my own part
Like real actors do
I'll make faces
Smile
Have all eyes on me
Who needs the main part
When you can be a tree?

Baby Sister

Trees in the churchyard
stand in line,
guarding this little
sister of mine.
My baby sister died
inside Mum's tummy.
She will always be my sister
and Mum will always be her mummy.

Aaron the Rat

My brother Fred
has named his pet rat after me!
He calls,
"Come on, Aaron,
it's time for your tea!

Come on, Aaron,
show-time, mate!
Practise your tricks,
make no mistakes!"

When Fred isn't looking
I'll set Aaron free,
back to his home,
to his rodent family.

Then I'll replace him
with a mouse instead.
What shall I call him?
How about
Fred?

The Twins

I see my sister
You see my twin
I see a person
The person within.
You see a face
Exactly the same
I see my sister
Let me explain...
We shared the same womb
But don't share a heart
We don't share a mind
We were born apart.
We are not 'the twins'
We don't share a name
Are our characters different?
Oh dear, not again!
Just like you and your sibling
We are each ourselves
There's no need for questions
No need to delve
I see my sister
You see my twin
Is it too much to ask
To see the person within?

Moon to Share

I rest my eyes upon our moon
When we are far apart
Knowing your moon is my moon
Soothes my aching heart

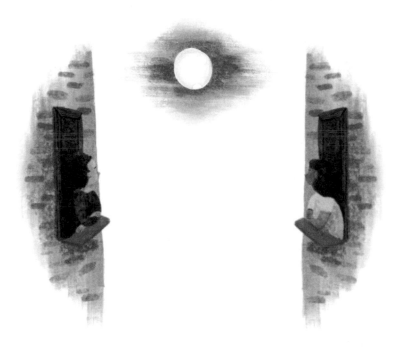

*Isn't it amazing and wonderful to think that everyone
in the world shares the same moon?
Next time you're missing someone, ask them to look up
at the moon the same time as you.*

Serial Shopper

Dad's in trouble with Mum again,
she's mad, she's cross, she's hopping.
She sent him out for a dozen eggs –
he came back with NINE bags of shopping!

The freezer is full to bursting,
the fridge is groaning away.
All the food that Dad has bought
has a use-by date of today!

Buy me now or lose me forever!
Buy one, get the other half-price!
How long does it take to eat
twelve bags of basmati rice?

Last week it was three dozen nappies –
my youngest brother is seven.
Ten tins of pedigree dog food –
it's years since Scamp went to heaven!

Then one day Dad started whistling.
We really feared the worst.
He didn't seem like Dad at all,
excited enough to burst.

First he astonished our mother
with a big bouquet of flowers.
Then he proudly announced his exciting news...
he could now shop 24 hours!

Lily

Lily's mum and dad live in Hollywood
They make films we see on the screen
She says her dad drives an Aston Martin
Her mum's chauffeured in a limousine

Lily's mum wants her to move there
But she says she'll miss her friends
Her dad flies his luxury jet
To fetch her some weekends

At the moment she lives with her grandma
She says her real house is by the sea
In a huge clifftop mansion
With views of the yachts by the quay

Lily's gran is lovely
She kisses her goodbye at the gate
She waits with a smile at home-time
She's never, ever late

Her gran's house is tiny
Her bedroom is the size of a box
With just enough room for her bed
A small chest for her pants and socks

Lily's garden is weeny
But although there's not much space
It's full of beautiful flowers
It's a very special place

I've never seen Lily's mansion
Or her dad's luxury jet
Sometimes I think I'll ask to
But then, I just forget.

Love Is Never Lost

(For Uschi and Angelika)

The rose said to her petals,
"Are you leaving me forever?"
"No," said the petals.
"Those we love
never lose each other.
Never."

Kindness

Kindness is like a boomerang
Thrown into the air
Watch it fly and spin
Spreading kindness everywhere
Then watch it catch you by surprise
As it heads back down your way

Spread a little kindness
Throw your boomerang today!

Creature Baby!

Mum's stomach is BIG.
She says there's a baby inside
but I think my mum's been 'had',
the doctors and nurses have lied!

Aargh! It's HUGE!
It's ENORMOUS!
What if it's
A STEGOSAURUS?

Or a bear in there,
or it could be a tiger,
maybe a whale or a dolphin
inside her!

Aargh! It's HUGE!
It's ENORMOUS!
What if it's
A STEGOSAURUS?

Or an elephant,
giraffe, or giant shark,
or a terrifying dog
with a vicious bark!

Aargh! It's HUGE!
It's ENORMOUS!
What if it's
A STEGOSAURUS?

On reflection, perhaps,
wouldn't it be cool
to be the most popular
kid in school?

Arriving each morning
with a Creature in tow,
I'd be that child
they'd all want to know.

They'd fight to sit next to me,
to be my best mate,
bring in sweets and treats,
tell me I'm great.

So...

If it's HUGE
If it's ENORMOUS
If it IS a STEGOSAURUS...

WOW!!

Eilag Nilletemythguan

There once was a man called Eilag Nilletemythguan
Who lived a long time ago
Alone on a remote island in the Pacific
Eilag Nilletemythguan had
Two pairs of eyes in the back of his head
So he could see the past and the future every day
Three noses so he could smell an ant from fifty miles
Three mouths so he could eat all the day's meals
   at once
Which left more time for his favourite hobby,
   singing
Eilag Nilletemythguan sang to the fish out in
   the ocean
To the fluff in his beard and to the twitch in his
   middle finger
Eilag Nilletemythguan lived to one hundred
   and twelve...
Or does his name suggest otherwise?

Is this story true or false? Clue: The answer is hidden in his name...!

Not Just a Cloud

Right, children.
Clouds.
Look up.
What can you see?
I see Cumulus clouds...

Wow! I see a pirate ship, sir,
moving really slowly through foamy white waves.
That bit looks like a skull-and-crossbones flag, sir.

Cumulus clouds are...

Look! That one's a prehistoric fish, sir!
I can see its fangs, sir, look!

formed of water droplets.

Or an old man's beard!
It's Father Christmas, sir!

Cumulus clouds are around
one kilometre wide.

Now there's a spaceship, sir!

With a flat base.

Angel wings!
Wow, sir!
Look at that angel, it's beautiful!

Right, break-time!
Test on Cumulus facts afterwards.
We'll see who's been listening, shall we?

Moving On

Take me back to the other house
The one they're calling 'old'
With the sycamore tree in the garden
Where the sign outside says SOLD

The name on my door said
Holly's Room
Not anyone else's name
My walls were blue
Not grey like these
Here, it's just not the same

But when I remember Mum's words
I don't feel quite so alone
It's the tears of love and laughter
That make a house a home

We'll make enough new memories
To fill a treasure chest
Memories we'll keep forever
Of times we'll never forget.

Worm

Worm popped up
from the garden soil.
Mouse,
Why do you sit here, so?

I sit to watch
the flowers bloom,
the seasons come and go.

Tosh! said the worm.
You are missing out,
come on down below.
Where you sit is the end of it all.
Want to see the start of the show?

Mouse followed worm way down deep,
burrowed through the darkest hole.
Arrived at the bottom to watch the seeds...

then got eaten by a mole!

Blackberry Picking

Leave me the ones
That are just out of reach
The ones entangled by thorns
Shielded by skin-ripping brambles
By a field of freshly cut corn

Leave me the ones
That are just out of reach
The ones worth fighting for
I'll battle the tall nettle soldiers
A sting or two or more

Leave me the ones
That are just out of reach
Plump and black as tar
For those which prove the hardest to grasp
Are the sweetest tasting, by far.

Callum's Homework

Dear Miss Price,

This story sounds unbelievable
but every word is true.
My poor Callum just finished his homework
when out of the window it flew!

Over the wall to Miss Buttons,
across her award-winning veg,
on top of her dustbins and under her car.
Got stuck in her hawthorn hedge!

As Callum reached out to grab it –
whoosh! The paper again took flight.
Callum gave chase for miles and miles.
His homework was now a kite!

Then! My Callum spotted his homework
on top of the village church spire.
There gathered an anxious crowd below
as my Callum climbed higher and higher!

Poor Callum had to admit defeat
as the homework took off again,
over the sea to the Isle of Wight,
to Ireland or France or Spain!

There is only one word for my Callum, Miss Price,
a HERO, through and through.
The story of my Callum's homework is
unbelievable, but true.

From
My Mum

IF

'*If!*' You are a word that could do with a holiday!
It must be exhausting being you, *If*,
Mum says your name all the time.
'IF you don't have an ice cream after school on Friday
you could have one at the park on Sunday.
IF we're really, really careful with money this week
we could have pizza for tea on Saturday.
IF we don't spend any money today
or tomorrow
we might be able to take the bus to see Grandad.'
Oh, *If!*
And me?
IF my school uniform gets any tighter
IF my school trousers get any shorter
IF I put jam on my shoes
my trousers might come down for tea!
Seriously, *If*,
you're overworked,
you're overused,
but you know
You're pretty priceless.
Because without you, *If*,
There would be no such thing as
HOPE.

Morning Song

Hear the morning wake
Water bubbles in the kettle
Chink of the lid on the teapot
Rattle of a tea cup
Clunk of the toaster
Outside
Five birds on a wire
Sing their own morning song

Dear Mrs Bright

Dear Mrs Bright,

There's a school down the road
It needs a new Head
I've seen the advert online
Needs to be:
Loyal (tick!)
Dynamic (tick!)
With a calm and focused mind (tick!)

Wow! That's YOU, Mrs Bright!

Organised (tick!)
Assertive (tick!)
Clear (tick!)
Compassionate (tick!)
Kind (tick!)
Sincere (tick!)

Wow! That's YOU, Mrs Bright!

PLEASE, Mrs Bright...
consider applying
They'd be lucky to have you
I'm not lying

Because, Mrs Bright
It really is torture
Being one of your pupils
And also your daughter!

With the kindest ever regards,

Ellie Bright

Kite

Wait for me, kite!
Let me glide with you
Swoop and soar
Into the hot blueness
Of a summer sky

Catching the wind
As it blows southwards
Over fields of ripe golden corn
Over oxeye daises
In rippling grasses

Wait for me, kite!
Let me blow with you
Over church steeples
Red roofs and pine trees
Over reedy banks
Crystal clear rivers

Let's ride the wind
As it waltzes us up into
The blue
Way, way
Above the haze of cloud
And beyond.

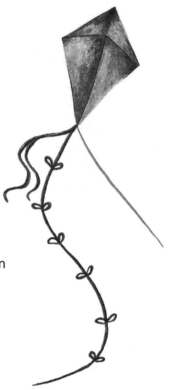

Sleepover Gran

Gran rings me up,
I hear her say,
"How about a sleepover?
Can I come today?"
Then in she walks
with her overnight case,
toothpaste and toothbrush,
excited face.
"What are we watching?"
She looks at the telly.
"Something spooky and scary
that will turn us to jelly!"
Then she tips out a bag
of the stickiest sweets,
green, pink and blue ones
Mum never lets me eat.
Sleepover Gran,
best sleepover friend.
I never want sleepovers
with Gran to end.

Love Heart

I drew a love heart
Just for you
In winter's icy snow
But the warmth of my love
Melted it
So now you'll never know

The World Speaks

I, The World, need listeners.
People, do you hear what I say?
Would any listeners please line up,
I need to speak with you today!

Please stop your laughter and your fun.
Please stop your endless chatter.
I need your help, pay attention please,
your World is a serious matter.

Aha! At last we have silence.
You listeners have found a way.
You walked quietly past the raucous crowd
to join your World today.

Your ability to listen,
your calm and focused minds,
will guide us through life's challenges.
The World so needs your kind.

Now we have come together,
my do-ers and talkers, too.
The World can be a better place,
thanks to all of you.

What Am I?

My first is in asteroid
Not in rock
My second in Space
Not in dock

Third is in orbit
Not in stars
Fourth is in landing
Not in Mars

Fifth is in light-year
Not in away
Next is in Moon
Not Milky Way

My last is a number
Which rhymes with heaven
Just one clue
It is not number seven.

Miss

Miss wasn't there this morning
Our Head met us at the door
Things felt strange
I didn't like it
Then Miss arrived
Our lovely Miss
Miss with puffy eyes
Miss with a very sad face
Head said
We all had to be especially good
Because Miss had a headache
But no one was good
Lucy kicked Saniyah's chair
Elliot wouldn't stop talking
Aleksander kept rocking the table
Miss's voice got quieter and quieter
Until it was just a whisper
At break
I took my cake from my lunch box
Placed it on her desk
And went out to play

Experiment Day

Today is an Experiment
A trial day to see
If I am able to improve
This present version of ME

ME is nice
I am fond of ME
But is ME the BEST EVER
ME that I could be?

I will listen today
Focus, talk less
Ask Dad about work
I won't say it's a test

I'll ring Grandad up
Make his day
Should I mention *'experiment'*?
Perhaps best not to say

I'll water the plants
Do it all with a smile
Dad mustn't guess
Today is a trial

If I try really hard
Will Dad like what he sees?
The new and improved
Version of ME?

Wish Upon a Star

What happens to wishes
when we wish upon a star?
Are they cuddled, tickled, sung to?
Are they kept inside a jar?

What happens to wishes?
Are they put to bed?
Are they read a story?
Or can they stay up instead?

What happens to wishes?
I'd really like to know.
If I wish upon a star,
where do my wishes go?

Blue Moon Haiku

Blue moon floating high
You have been away too long
Oh, how I've missed you

A Haiku is a form of Japanese poetry, written entirely of 17 syllables with three lines of 5, 7 and 5 syllables. Why don't you try writing one?

Pound on the Ground

I found a pound on the ground.
Steven and Habiba said it wasn't found,
it was stolen.
They said I stole it,
that I should have given it in.
I did give it in –
just not straight away,
because for one whole morning
I felt the weight of that pound,
a shiny gold pound
in my trouser pocket,
which could be mine
if I chose.

At play
Fatima called me a thief.
Molly said I thieved.
They both said thieves couldn't be trusted.
No one trusted me to play with them.

My pocket was empty now
so how come something
ten times the weight of that pound
was pushing me down?

Then at break
they were pointing at me.
A boy from Year 5
headed my way,
followed by half my class.
"Hey, you!" he shouted.

He'd heard about the pound.
He'd heard I was a thief.
He'd heard I couldn't be trusted.
I'd heard he was a bully.

"Hey!" he shouted again.
His eyes met mine.
"That pound you found?
It was mine.
Thanks, kid."

King Cat

Our cat doesn't use the cat flap
He requests someone open the door
Cat flaps are for moggies, he says
Cat flaps are such a bore

Our cat doesn't eat from a cat bowl
He sits at the table with pride
Napkin around his furry neck
Eating his cat food deep-fried

Our cat doesn't mew 'hello'
He gives us the royal wave
A twist of his paw to his subjects
How else should a blue-blood behave?

Our cat doesn't sleep on his cushion
He sleeps in a huge double bed
In his sardine-patterned PJs
Feather pillow for his sleepy head

Our cat does like admirers
Who visit specially to chat
About this royal resident
Our very own King Cat!

Animal Riddle

My first is in Hamster and not in Mouse
My second is in Pigeon and also in Grouse
My third is in Hound and not in Cat
My fourth is in Gerbil and not in Rat
My fifth is in Elk and also in Moose
My sixth is in Chicken and not in Goose
My seventh is in Vole and not in Shrew
My last is in Goat and also Gnu!

Answer: (Hedgehog)

Home for Uncle Len

Uncle Len
lives in a Home
he imagines is afloat.
He calls the staff
'The crew',
like they all live on a boat.

"Batten down the hatches!"
he'll call when it's stormy outside.
Walks each day from bow to stern
with dignity and pride.

Uncle Len's forgotten his wife's name.
He can't remember his own.
But it's true that a sailor never forgets
the place they once called home.

*Uncle Len is suffering from a disease called Alzheimer's, which affects
a person's memory and ability to think and function as they used to.
Sometimes, a person suffering with Alzheimer's disease may appear
to live in the past, like Uncle Len.*

Empty Chair

Today will be a long one.
My best friend Amir is away.
The seat beside me is empty
and I'm really worried about play.

I don't like the noise of screeching
or shoving and pushing around.
I'll hide myself till the bell goes,
somewhere away from the crowd.

The next big worry is lunchtime.
Where shall I stand in the queue?
Who will I sit by to eat my lunch?
Such a long day to get through.

Now I know how Amir feels
when sometimes I'm not there.
Lonely, worried and anxious,
beside an empty chair.

A Poppy for Albert Davies

Albert Davies wears a poppy
On Remembrance Day each year
And in the two-minutes' silence
He wipes away a tear
He says one day he'll tell us
Of when and where and why
What his poppy means to him
And why it makes him cry

Many men and women who contributed in various ways to war find their experiences difficult to speak about, although their memories stay ever fresh in their minds. Remembrance Sunday, when they wear a poppy to remember those who died, will always be special to them.

Earth to Intensive Care

Breaking news!
Our precious Planet Earth
Is fighting for its life tonight
Its symptoms are serious
Severe congestion
Shortness of breath
Soaring temperature
It's not looking good, folks
We'll be here all night
Stay with us
Bleep
Bleep

Breaking news!
The world's best surgeons
Are operating on Earth right now
Earth is said to be in a critical condition
We'll be here throughout
To give you more news as it comes in
Bleep
Bleep

Breaking news!
Earth is now out of Theatre
But remains critical in Intensive Care
Bleep
Bleep

Breaking news!
Earth is now breathing on its own
However
Surgeons removed
Oceans of toxic plastic we didn't need to buy
Harmful greenhouse gases we helped create
I could go on....

What saved Earth's life?

Acorns, millions of them
I have the prescription here, folks
It reads:
'Essential for recovery and long-term health
Acorns and seeds to grow trees
As many as we can plant
Trees-mean-breath-mean-life'
They don't want us to ever forget that
The hard work must never stop
If we look after Earth
Earth will look after us.

What can I say, folks?
It's been emotional
We almost lost our Earth tonight
Let's not find ourselves here again
Ever
Thanks for watching.

Change of Direction

yrteoP si a drib
tI swonk on reitnorf
fI uoy
kooL, hctaw, netsil
dnA raeh
noitaripsnI si erehwyreve
nI yreve tnemevom
yrevE erats
rehtaG sdrow
nipS meht dnuora
daeR meht duola
raeH woh yeht dnuos
etirW morf eht traeh
etirW ruoy yaw
uoY yam eb a dehsilbup
teoP eno yad.

Each word is written backwards. 'Poetry is a bird...'

A Star Called Christa

There is an asteroid named Christa
And a crater on the moon
In memory of a teacher
Who lost her life too soon

Christa was so excited
To have won the coveted place
The first US civilian
To venture into space

Millions of children watched in schools
Millions of children cried
As seventy-three seconds after launch
The dream that was hers had died

There must be a star called Christa
A star that will never die
Beaming a ray of love and hope
To dreamers like you and I.

In memory of Christa McAuliffe who died on the Challenger
Space Shuttle Mission on 28th January, 1986

Grief

Grief can catch you
Like fishermen
Catch fish
Caught in a net
By surprise
You're reeled in
Captured
Then sometimes
You're thrown
Back into the sea
To swim

How NOT to Impersonate Your Mum on the Telephone!

Swimming
The worst day of the week
Mum refused to write a note
So...

I practised in the mirror
The facial expression
That high-pitched screeching whine
"My Benjamin is so ill today!"
"My Benjamin has such a fever!"

I looked like Mum
I sounded like Mum
I *was* Mum!
So...

Picked up the telephone...
Dialled the number...
Deep breath and...
"Hello!
This is my mum speaking!"

Oops!

Forest Secrets

A jewel-encrusted treasure chest
A thousand years old and a day
Rests beneath an oak tree
Where chattering children play

The silver horn of a unicorn
Its mane of snowy-white
Lie beside a woody glade
Where badgers play at night

Fairy wings of gossamer
Flash through trees of green
Dancing in the moonlight
Heard but rarely seen

The wonders of the forest
Are buried safe and deep
No one knows their secret
That is yours and mine
    to keep

Tomorrow

Today
Has not been great
I'll put it in a box
Tomorrow is another chance
To shine

This short poem is called a Cinquain.
Cinquains consist of 5 lines of 2,4,6,8 and 2 syllables.
Why not try writing your own?

Poetry Is Everywhere

Moonbeams on a starry night
Sunlight through a door ajar
A gust of wind on a breezy day
The sound of a flute from afar

A footprint on the freshest snow
The sight of a leaping hare
Patter of rain on a window
The smell of after-rain air

A look of love from a loved one
Discovering a forgotten place
A rolling tear of sadness
The feel of a warm embrace

In the dancing flames of a fire
In the sweetness of a golden pear
No need to search for poetry

It is with you everywhere.

Thanks

Special thanks to poet and editor Brian Moses for his generous support and encouragement throughout the years. Brian gave me the confidence to realise my dream of becoming a published writer. And here I am.

Also to poet and editor Roger Stevens for publishing my very first poem in 2013 and for his continual support.

Thanks to my 'writing family' on social media, whose encouragement has meant so much. In particular, poets Neal Zetter, Joshua Seigal, Sarah Ziman, James Carter and Julie Stevens.

Sincere thanks to Executive Headteacher David Coaché and Headteacher Hayley Potter and their wonderful staff at Bengeworth CE Academy, Evesham, for their love of poetry and for allowing us all to push poetry boundaries.

To my wonderful Bengeworth Festival pupils who have brought so much joy to my teaching.

Thank you to young Thomas Clelland for sitting at my poetry table one day and asking 'Where's your book, Miss?' You sowed the seed! Also to the lovely novelist Kate Mallinder, whose tenacity is my inspiration every day.

To Janetta Otter-Barry, Arianna Osti and the brilliant team at Otter-Barry Books. Their very special insight has created a wonderful book. Thank you, Janetta, for being an absolute joy to work with. To the magical pen of the brilliantly talented Illustrator Jess Mason who has truly brought these poems to life.

Lastly, to my husband and daughters, my most constructive critics and champions!

Acknowledgements

A Star Called Christa first published in *Spaced Out,* edited by Brian Moses and James Carter, Bloomsbury, 2019

Callum's Homework first published in *The Best Ever Book of Funny Poems,* edited by Brian Moses, Macmillan Children's Books, 2021

Forest Secrets first published in *Fire Burn, Cauldron Bubble,* edited by Paul Cookson, Bloomsbury, 2020

Grandad's Leaving Home first published in *Caterpillar* magazine, 2015

Grief first published in *Is this a Poem?,* edited by Roger Stevens, Bloomsbury, 2016

How NOT to Impersonate Your Mum on the Telephone! first published in *I Bet I can Make you Laugh,* edited by Joshua Seigal, Bloomsbury, 2018

Read Me Backwards! first published in *I Am a Jigsaw,* edited by Roger Stevens, Bloomsbury, 2019

What Am I? first published in *Moonstruck!,* edited by Roger Stevens, Otter-Barry Books, 2019

DEBRA BERTULIS

has been writing all her life. She is a poet, story writer and staged playwright. Though it is poetry which has been a constant companion and her greatest passion.

Her poems have been widely anthologised by some of the UK's best-known poets, performed at festivals worldwide and included on the LAMDA examination syllabus.

She has 'the best job in the world', visiting schools and libraries, enabling children of all abilities to engage with poetry and to become poets themselves. She lives in Herefordshire with her family.

JESS MASON

studied Illustration at the University of Worcester. She graduated with a First in 2018 and also won the Otter-Barry Books Narrative Illustration Award. She is drawn to stories and poems containing adventure, humour and fantasy. Jess takes inspiration from folk art, medieval manuscripts, Renaissance maps and film to create illustrations that are characterful and atmospheric, using a combination of hand-rendered and digital processes. She lives in Worcester.